Craig Raine was born in Shildon, Co. Durham, in 1944. He was educated at Exeter College, Oxford. After teaching at various O*Quarto* in 1979 and wa *New Statesman*. He is c Faber. His books of pc *A Martian Sends a Postc* His libretto for Nigel C *the Soviet Union*, was p *Prophetic Book* was published in a limited edition by Correspondance des Arts, Lodz. Craig Raine is also the editor of *A Choice of Kipling's Prose* (Faber).

He lives in Oxford with his wife, Ann Pasternak Slater, and their four children.

by the same author

THE ONION, MEMORY (OUP)
A MARTIAN SENDS A POSTCARD HOME (OUP)
RICH
THE ELECTRIFICATION OF THE
SOVIET UNION

CRAIG RAINE

'1953'

A version of Racine's Andromaque

faber and faber
LONDON · BOSTON

First published in 1990
by Faber and Faber Limited
3 Queen Square London WC1N 3AU

Photoset by Wilmaset Birkenhead Wirral
Printed in Great Britain by
Richard Clay Ltd Bungay Suffolk

All rights reserved

© Craig Raine, 1990

Craig Raine is hereby identified
as author of this work in accordance with
Section 77 of the Copyright, Designs and Patents Act 1988.

This book is sold subject to the condition that it shall not, by way of trade or otherwise, be lent, resold, hired out or otherwise circulated without the publisher's prior consent in any form of binding or cover other than that in which it is published and without a similar condition including this condition being imposed on the subsequent purchaser.

A CIP record for this book is available from the British Library
ISBN 0-571-14312-1

DRAMATIS PERSONAE

KLAUS MARIA VON ORESTES
Hitler's secret envoy in Rome, sent to claim Angus LeSkye's life as a potential danger to German interests, and to persuade Vittorio Mussolini to marry the German princess, Ira. Orestes, however, loves Ira himself.

OLDENBURG
German ambassador to Rome and an old friend of von Orestes.

VITTORIO MUSSOLINI
Son of Benito Mussolini and King of Italy. In love with his English prisoner, the widowed Lady LeSkye, but pledged to marry Princess Ira.

FENICE
Personal adviser to Vittorio Mussolini and formerly to Benito Mussolini. In his late fifties, but vigorous.

ANNETTE LESKYE
Widow of Hector LeSkye, mother of Angus LeSkye who is a claimant to the English throne.

KATE
Old family servant of the LeSkye family. More like a lady-in-waiting than a menial.

PRINCESS IRA
Former lover of von Orestes, but now officially engaged to Vittorio Mussolini, whom she loves.

EBERHARD
Male servant–companion of Princess Ira.

ACT ONE

Scene 1

The set in total darkness. From the very back of the stage to the front, two guards do the passo romano *down each side of the stage, turn right and left, meet stage front, and change the guard. They wear the usual fascist woks. A walkway ensures that their noise is magnified. It should sound and look like the changing of the guard at the Neue Wache on Unter den Linden. When it is over, they march back, having changed positions. The set is illuminated dimly as they pass it on their way to the brick wall, where one remains a presence, however distant, throughout the proceedings. This ritual is repeated at the beginning of every act, except Act Four. I assume a curtain at the end of every act.*

The set can now be seen as a grubby underground bureaucracy of green filing cabinets, military desks, caged light bulbs, sheeted furniture, metal wastepaper bins, out-trays arranged like pagodas, box files, metal bookshelves, typewriters. These form a horseshoe or three sides of a square around the central playing area – a slightly raked chess board, the tiled reception area of a semi-ruined Italian palazzo. The general effect should be of a classical ruin set down in office detritus.

COUNT KLAUS MARIA VON ORESTES *is presenting his credentials to the German ambassador,* HERR OLDENBURG. *The* COUNT *wears the uniform of a general in the Waffen SS. He carries a leather portfolio and is decorated with the Iron Cross. He displays an unpredictable turn and slight toss of the head – a motor defect.*

The AMBASSADOR *wears an elegant suit which, thanks to his plumpness, is just a little too tight.*

ORESTES

(*He clicks his heels and salutes.*)
>General Count Klaus Maria von Orestes,
>seconded from the Eastern front
>to act as the Führer's special envoy.

OLDENBURG

(*Springing open a cigarette case.*)
>Heil Hitler. Look, Klaus, I'll be blunt.
>You and I, we're old friends, aren't we?
>Gasper? This is how things stand:
>yes, Vittorio's conduct is, of course,
>an insult to the Fatherland
>and all that, but what can we actually do?
>Oh sure, we can *threaten* war.
>At least rhetoric isn't in short supply.
>We've spares of *that*, and then some more.

ORESTES

(*Unzips his portfolio.*)
>Please read them. My instructions from Berlin.
>As loyal servants to the state,
>we do our duty. We follow orders.
>There can be no manoeuvre, no debate.
>Our personal opinions are irrelevant.

OLDENBURG

(*Reads a moment in silence.*)
>A skinny, freckled boy must die.
>Because he could inherit the English throne.
>The evil eight-year-old. LeSkye.
>I see. Will we torture him first, Klaus?
>Your orders should have spelt that out,
>referred us to whatever the standard manual is.
>Like this, it leaves a nasty doubt:

to beat or not to beat. Sorry. Sorry.
A year of this, you'd be the same.
Cynical. Now, what's next? The marriage?
Yes: Ira takes Vittorio's name,
as arranged before. Very neat. Well planned –
again. The princess will be pleased.
And you're indifferent to her now: right?
All passion spent?

(*No answer from* ORESTES.)

Kaput?

ORESTES
Deceased?
(*His head jerks. He tries to mask the tic as a head-shake, then smiles at the pretence.*)
Can you order a nerve not to twitch?
Ban it by edict of the state?
No, I still love her. In the body politic,
my heart is insubordinate.

OLDENBURG
But what about all your letters,
Klaus? Were they just a pack of lies,
like the fibs of a secret drinker?
Perhaps I shouldn't be surprised,
but I am. Christ, how can you bear the boredom
of being nothing else but thirst?
Thirst and a dry ache of atoms,
your lips perpetually pursed . . .

ORESTES

(*Interrupts.*)
>and wanting her wetness, and then her wetness again?
>That's it. I lied. I told myself
>that I'd come through the fire. Cauterized.
>As sturdy as a pot from Delft.
>You're my oldest friend. Since the Gymnasium.

(*Pause. Their eyes meet and drop immediately.*)

>I never meant to lie to you.
>I could feel my heart harden. Like a muscle.
>The things I wrote I thought were true.
>When this whole thing started, you were . . . What?
>Averse? But sympathetic, no?

OLDENBURG

>To you. And when the Führer offered Ira to
>that shaved baboon, Vittorio,
>for mass murder in the Axis cause, I had
>to talk you out of suicide.

ORESTES

>A cunt for an arsehole. The perfect match,
>you said, appealing to my pride.
>And it worked. For a bit it really worked.
>I'd sit with vodka in my tank
>at Stalingrad and imagine details:
>you know, a collarbone, a flank,
>its touch and go in her dress,
>but then I'd laugh this weird laugh
>and pull her to pieces in my head,
>as if I were a psychopath.
>I was convinced I was completely cured.

OLDENBURG

(*Grimaces.*)
    Let's skip that bit. Then what? Renown.
    The iron cross. Back to Berlin as Hitler's hero.

ORESTES

(*Nodding*)
    When all the Reichstag members yelled
    for Vittorio Mussolini's guts,
    can you imagine what I felt?

OLDENBURG

A certain *Schadenfreude*?

ORESTES

No. What I felt was ecstasy.
Vittorio had gone too far. In his palace, here,
our ally had the boy LeSkye.
Hector's son. Half Jewish. Part Bowes-Lyon.
And claimant to the British throne.
But dead, we thought. A Gestapo funeral.
No flowers, and forget the stone.
Wrong. Lady LeSkye had arranged a switch,
so Himmler gave some other kid
his *exeat*. Back of the neck and buried.

OLDENBURG

While shaking little Angus hid.
You should see him. The boy's no threat.

ORESTES
The boy. The boy. That's not the point.
I couldn't care less about the boy.
I wanted Hitler to appoint
me as a way of reaching Ira again.
I lobbied everyone I knew.
Just everyone. The worst shits you could imagine.
I stood – I *knelt* in every queue
to kiss important arses. And got the job:
because I had to get her back
before Vittorio changed his mind.

OLDENBURG
Like points switched on a railway track.
Or something else ponderously mechanical.
He's brave perhaps, but hardly bright,
our Vittorio.

ORESTES
But why *doesn't* he marry Ira?

OLDENBURG
Well now, the postponed wedding night.
The Führer is said to be displeased.
This insult to the bride-to-be,
a German bride-to-be, was calculated
to shock his sense of chivalry.
Too bad. It's simple: Vittorio loves
her ladyship, Annette LeSkye.
But don't expect him to renounce Ira.
He won't. However hard you try.

ORESTES
He doesn't want to disrupt the alliance?

OLDENBURG
It's partly that, but mostly this:
maybe intellect isn't his strength;
his feelings, though, you can't dismiss
them in the same way. Not at all. They *are* strong.
His balls are bigger than his brains.
So when Lady LeSkye responds coolly,
his overtures always change.
He gets nasty. Threatens the boy.
Reduces her to tears. And shouts
a lot. He's good at that: that and losing control.
But when he throws his weight about,
the momentum takes him back to Ira.
So please don't ask me what he'll do.
The man is toxic with testosterone.

ORESTES
Of course. I know that feeling, too.
It's love. Real love. Love as a long terror.
It isn't civilized, or kind.
But necessary. Callous. Felt and inflicted.
Endured, embraced. Enlightened, blind.
Does Ira complain much about her treatment?

OLDENBURG
No. Outwardly, she stays aloof.
Every centimetre the Hohenzollern princess.
But all her breeding isn't proof
against Vittorio's emotional assault course.
Sometimes you see her swollen eyes.
She talks about leaving but somehow she stays on.
She's mentioned you. Yes. Once or twice.
The knight in the shining armoured car
is how I think she thinks of you.
At least when you aren't actually there.

ORESTES
Always the ironist. If you only knew
how childish it sounds to someone like me,
this antiseptic sanity
of yours, you wouldn't bother to waste it.
I'm proud to have no vanity.

OLDENBURG
My old friend. My old, old friend. Still the same . . .

(*Puts out his hand to touch* ORESTES, *but sees* VITTORIO *approaching and announces in an official voice:*)

Herr General, here comes the King.
(*Adding in an undertone*)
Insist. Demand the boy with menaces.
Be bellicose, Teutonic. Sting
him into shielding his beloved Lady LeSkye.
That duty done, the way is clear
for you to prosecute your own affairs.

ORESTES
(*Nodding*)
Tell Princess Ira that I'm here.

(*Both men have been moving on to the central playing area, which they reach at 'toxic with testosterone'. Now* OLDENBURG *exits and* ORESTES *waits for* VITTORIO.)

Scene 2

VITTORIO *is in cavalry uniform: Ionian white with lashings of gold. Boots, spurs, jodhpurs. He flexes a swagger stick and uses it to swat the air menacingly. In looks, he resembles Ernest Borgnine: gat-toothed, a heavy beard kept clean-shaven, hatless, hair-oiled.*

FENICE, *his personal adviser, wears civilian clothes. He is an unawed provincial in his middle to late fifties. Not a broad regional accent. Like Geoffrey Boycott, say.*

Though not drunk, VITTORIO *and* FENICE *have been drinking. Both treat* ORESTES *casually. Perhaps as a consequence of* VITTORIO'S *consciousness of his absolute power.*

ORESTES

(*Neutral tone, but deliberately provocative*)
>Von Orestes. Sent to Rome by the Führer
>to represent the German race,
>the Reich which will last a thousand years,
>while lesser nations leave no trace.

FENICE

(*Not quite* sotto voce)
>Germany calling. This is Germany calling.

ORESTES

(*Icily*)
>In the features of his son,
>granite, larger than life, I perceive that
>the father's pedigree lives on.
>Of all this great city's memorials, fashioned
>from marble, bronze, obsidian, gold,
>you alone commemorate his flesh and blood:
>heroic in that outsize mould.

Your majesty, why did London surrender?
Because you changed the face of war,
with gas, carpet bombing, mass reprisals,
phosphorus, the anthrax spore.
Your father was famous for military deeds.
You were his son. You killed a city.
Realizing that warfare, modern warfare,
no longer had a place for pity,
your triumph was total. Like your techniques.
Nothing escaped. You murdered grass.
You poisoned water. Like some cataclysm,
not like a man, you came to pass.
Now we ask: why? Why have you weakened?
Germany wants this son to die
for all her sons, and her sons of sons, who fell,
defending Europe from LeSkye.
One day, sooner than you think, this brat
will seek revenge on all of us
in turn. But he'll probably start here in Rome.
Don't trust him. He'll betray your trust.
Like father, like son: the family business
survives until that boy is dead.
Hector LeSkye and Son. Butchers by appointment,
to yours and every royal head.

VITTORIO

I thought you'd come about something important,
like reparations, or a loan.
Orestes. Plus retinue. By submarine. My God,
we could have settled this by phone.
Is Germany serious? Little Angus? *Angus*.
His second teeth, watch out for them.
Germ warfare, too. Whooping cough, mumps,

colds, measles – deadly stratagems.
Fenice, explain this to me, would you?
They call themselves the Fatherland.
Will they adopt this mite without a father?
(*Shakes his head slowly.*)
They want to kill him. Out of hand.
But it's none of their fucking business, is it?
Fenice, have you got that file?
In negotiations with our closest ally,
we keep accounts, book-keeping style.
I can dispose of Angus however I choose.
Your country has no claim on him.
Or on his mother. They're legitimate spoils.
I didn't seize them on a whim.
Watching what was left of London smoke
like earth in the morning sun,
we sat in conference all one long day,
until the bargaining was done.
I can remember the table. Our papers stirred
and shifted in the open air.
Peace. You could hear a pen scratch.
Fenice has the details there.

FENICE

Hostages. Trials of. Provision for.
Lord Kent to German custody.
Spencers ditto. Over the page. Yes.
Her ladyship to Italy.
Here: Annette LeSkye and dependants.

VITTORIO

I hope you're satisfied by that.
The Führer's concern is touching, but say

we don't expect a *coup d'état*
in the immediate future. Or the distant.
Once for all, the British Empire died.
On a million whitewashed flagpoles,
the Union Jack was struck worldwide
and one small boy can't revive that power.
It's gone. I promise. Gone for good.
You'd believe me if you'd seen the Thames
infuse and brighten with the blood
of all the bodies bobbing there like teabags.
War. There was a boy there with nothing on
except a pair of wellingtons.
When we hanged the little bugger, one fell off
into the road. His face went bronze.
Weird. The rest of him seemed very white.
I'm capable of being callous.
But on the battlefield, like any soldier.
Not in the Mussolini palace.
Not now. Poor Aberdeen Angus. The fatted calf.
These German butchers want your veal.

ORESTES

That phrase, 'Annette LeSkye and dependants',
excluded Angus from the deal
because all the signatories, even you,
believed he was already dead.
No one knew then that our officers
had killed a substitute instead.
Safe conduct never applied to him,
so we insist on his return

or German troops may march on Rome,
in strength, to see your city burn
and Panzers ride the rubble, tilting
like a fleet of battleships.

VITTORIO
Quite poetic for a threat, eh, Fenice?

FENICE
But fine words butter no parsnips
with us, do they? There's nothing in it, is there?

VITTORIO
(*To* ORESTES)
>He's right. It's bankrupt, just a stunt.
>Every last tittuping tank
>is tied up on the Russian front.
>All your crack troops cracked up long ago.

ORESTES
And that's the answer you return?
A total rift? Perhaps our bride can teach you
the lesson you refuse to learn
from me.

VITTORIO
(*Puts the knife in deliberately.*)
>She never talks politics in bed.

ORESTES
May I see the Princess Ira?

VITTORIO
Of course. Fenice, a permit for the Count.

FENICE
In a jiffy. Where's my Biro?

Scene 3

FENICE *scribbles a chit for* ORESTES, *who reads it, folds it away, then stiffly bows from the waist. While this is happening, a sentry marches towards stage front, about-turns, and returns to his original position.* IRA *is illuminated near the back of the stage and* ORESTES *heads in her direction.* FENICE *and* VITTORIO *watch* ORESTES.

FENICE
Wasn't there something between those two?

VITTORIO
The rumour was he loved her. Yes.

FENICE
Suppose it starts up: one look and, bingo,
they rediscover happiness.

VITTORIO
His hand in her hair. Reading her face
again and again all over again.
And her mouth half open. Like someone half asleep.
Joy that almost looks like pain.
Why not? It isn't hard to imagine it.
And I'd be like a dynamo
at rest at last. Suddenly still.

Why not? I'd give them leave to go
wherever they chose, whenever they chose.
Berlin, Bavaria.
(*Laughs.*)
          Bombay.
It would be such a relief, Fenice,
to tell you why. But not today.

Scene 4

As VITTORIO *says, 'to tell you why',* ANNETTE LESKYE *and* KATE *enter, threading through the concrete corridors. As* VITTORIO *addresses her, she stops, then joins him. He is disadvantaged in several ways and his behaviour vacillates between high-class shop assistant and uninhibited powerful barbarian.*

VITTORIO

Good afternoon. Can I help your ladyship
at all? Perhaps you wanted me?

ANNETTE

Thank you, no. I was on my way to my son,
now that once a day we're free,
for an hour, to sit crying together.
See for yourself. Cuddle up to the judas-hole
and watch your captives in their cell.
Reduced in stature. Reduced to tears.
Like bodies thrown into a well.
We've touched bottom and it's bottomless.
My son is all the little left
to me of his father, country, life itself.
I ask for mercy. From a depth

of misery so deep, I can't even be certain
that my request will reach your ears.

VITTORIO

Your request. Count Orestes brought another,
demanding payment of arrears
in the little matter of your son.

ANNETTE

When will they think we've paid enough?
My son doesn't even know who his father was.
Or what he meant. And I put off
telling him, knowing the knowledge
is dangerous. He's innocent.

VITTORIO

But your husband's son. And Jewish. The Nazis want
something they'd never document
or commit to paper. Hence the messenger,
the word of mouth. They want him dead.

ANNETTE

(*Flaring*)
    And of course you'll hand him over, won't you?
Nothing more that can be said
would make you change your mind, would it?
Deny you're jealous of the boy.
You can't. You think Angus is in your way.
This German business is a ploy.
But I don't believe anything you tell me.
If it were true, you could refuse:
you're not some puppet; you're an important ally.
You're lying.

VITTORIO
No. It's not a ruse.
They have actually threatened invasion,
should I decide I won't comply.
Well, I know precisely what to expect:
Luftwaffe squadrons in the sky,
neat as a military cemetery.
Flak, tracer, airborne troops. Defeat.
Strafed refugees diving like goalkeepers.
And when I give the order to retreat,
my own voice in the gas mask – like someone else's
cleft palate – sounding desperate.
Filthy, fatigued, but afraid to sleep:
who would be a head of state,
hearing the sea in one warm headphone,
while the stars fray and his eyes fill?
Me, apparently. Go on, I said. Invade.
The boy is mine, not yours to kill.
Lady LeSkye, consider my action carefully.
Consider what I've put at risk
in order to protect you and your son:
my country. Yes. The Führer won't go *tsk*
and brush all this aside. No. He'll mobilize.
I *am* your friend, and I regret
you think otherwise. The past is difficult,
I know. Some things, you *can't* forget.
And I don't ask forgiveness exactly either,
just that you try to understand
my position. Not now, but some time,
I ask the honour of your hand.
And your face, your lips, the way they move.

ANNETTE
The simple gesture simply made,
a king prepared to stoop to help the helpless,

is pure good. Without a shade.
Why adulterate this good with barter?
Defend a widow and her son
because they are without defenders;
because the weak have never won
before. Because the cause is just. It's enough.
My heart hobbles. You made it old.
You killed my husband. But, however much it aches,
at least it won't be bought or sold.
I am reserved. I am unbiddable.

VITTORIO

Unbending, too. That such a neck,
such a beautiful neck, should be so stiff.
I wasn't writing out a cheque,
or waving a stubby baton of bank notes,
or offering a tax-exempt
numbered Swiss bank account in Basle.
For that I might deserve contempt,
but not for pledging all Italy's resources.
Resources is too weak a word
for all those young men who will go out and die,
or come back, badly injured,
to their lives. Disfigured. Some in wheelchairs.
You've never seen an amputee?

(*He waits but she gives no indication either way.*)

The stump puckers like a kitbag. I once saw
a leg cut off above the knee.
Can you understand that, woman? Have you
   grasped
exactly what I'm offering?
If we win the war, I'll rebuild London,
free you, and crown your son its king.

ANNETTE
Your majesty, I'm not interested in majesty.
Perhaps I never was. My son
is, what? next to next in line – to danger.
I see the paid assassin's gun
stripped down on a hotel bed somewhere.
The stock, the telescopic sight,
the barrel, the silencer, the various parts,
all dormant in the bedside light
but primed with oil to penetrate the body.
And something else: a tower of change
leans there under the lamp, a few pfennigs.
Your majesty, this may sound strange,
but I should like to live in that tower,
in exile, well away from threats,
somewhere where the stakes are small.
Send us away now. Pay your debt
to Princess Ira. Marry her and save my son.

VITTORIO
I can't. Annette, you're killing me.
As coolly as some skivvy
might scald the racing circuitry
of household ants. But I'm not an insect
submissive to the general will.
I'm not some second secretary obliged
to use his diplomatic skill.
I love you, therefore I can't love her.
I am a king. I can ignore
the Führer, her love, my promises, anything.
I break and make the social law.

ANNETTE
But you can't ever order me to love you.
All powerful, your power stops there.
If you can't make yourself make love to Ira,
how can you banish my despair?

VITTORIO
I can't. But I can keep you here and add to it.
Unless you let me make you queen.

ANNETTE
You forget my husband. I can't forget him.
To marry you would be obscene.

VITTORIO
Thank you. A considered reply, I take it?
This interview is over now.
I suggest you go and visit your son
in gaol, before we have a row.
I wouldn't want you to see me lose my temper.
My temper can be violent.

(VITTORIO *rounds on* KATE. *He is audible without shouting.*)

So take your mistress off to the prison.
And quick. The patronizing cunt.
Or (see this swagger stick?) I'll fetch a ridge
up on her face she won't forget,
so next time she'll know who she's talking to.
Explain to her I'm not her vet,
or her gardener, or the fucking treasure who does.

(*He turns, completely in control, to* ANNETTE.)

Another word, your ladyship.
After so many, and so much talk, my last.
I think we've seen the balance tip.
You are so decided, I must be decided, too.
The boy will go to Germany.

ANNETTE

With a small suitcase and careful eyes. Yes.
But he won't arrive, will he?
The spare grey shirt, the washbag, the woven name
   tapes,
will disappear without a trace.
You want me to cry but I won't.

VITTORIO

Remember when you hold his face
that his head lies in your hands.

ACT TWO

Scene 1

The set is again illuminated by the withdrawal of the guard.
IRA *is having her hair dressed by* EBERHARD. *She is a blonde, quite formal in a tailored suit.* EBERHARD *stands behind her, hands on hips, holding a brush, waiting for an answer to some question.* IRA's *dark glasses give nothing away.*

EBERHARD *is difficult to place. His dialogue, but nothing else, gives away his sexual orientation. Otherwise, he is discreet in every way. An impeccable dark suit. A classless accent, except when he indulges in comic dialect mimicry – so good that we get a hint of his overlaid antecedents.*

EBERHARD
Drop Orestes then. Talk about something else.
(*Pause. Then broad Lancashire.*)
I think the Führer's hair is dyed.

IRA
(*Aria of irritation*)
Yes. Yes. Yes. Yes. Yes. Yes. Yes. Yes. Yes.
All right? I'll see him. Satisfied?
Just don't go on and on about him, that's all.
He wants to meet me? Fine.
And it's a good way of getting my own back on
that shit, Vittorio.

EBERHARD
Incline
your head a fraction this way, princess. Thank you.

IRA

I feel there's something not quite right.
About me seeing Orestes here. Of all places.
Don't worry, though. I'll be polite.

EBERHARD

Why on earth shouldn't you be, your highness?
Orestes is a paragon.
(*Broad Lancashire again*)
When that Mussolini screams so you can hear
the treble in his baritone,
and carries on like that at you,
we both of us think about Orestes. Oh yes
we do. Say what you like. It's true.
A gentleman. Not like some bloodsucking vampires
I could mention who deserve
a stake through their heart like a rollmop for
the way they've treated you. The nerve
of the man.
(*Normal voice*)
                But why feel shy with Orestes?

IRA

I feel embarrassed by the past.
(*Takes off her dark glasses and puts them in her bag. Lights a cigarette. Paces. Three puffs and stubs it out.*)
I threw him over without thinking I'd
be overthrown myself so fast.
I'd made another conquest. I gave the orders.
Orestes had his leave to go.

EBERHARD

Can we have you back here now? On the chair.
Shall I do that velvet bow?

IRA

(*Shakes her head.*)
> The months of humiliation were still to come.
> The full extent of my disgrace
> won't be felt, though, till my displaced suitor sees
> how well this princess knows her place.
> How smitten I really am. In so many places.

EBERHARD

> He won't take pleasure in your plight.
> He'll see it as a good chance to put himself
> in an even better light.
> You're close to a breakdown. You've been badly hurt.
> Your mind's as tender as a bruise.
> Orestes will be outraged and, honour bound,
> return Vittorio's abuse
> with interest, heap it on his oily head.
> What did the Führer's letter say?

IRA

> Either Vittorio marries me and hands over the boy,
> or I must leave, without delay.

EBERHARD

> Not to worry. Orestes'll know the latest,
> and tell us how the quarrel stands.
> Vittorio may have started this, but we'll finish it.
> And not with formal reprimands
> either, delivered through diplomatic channels.
> Revenge. We need to think ahead
> and outmanoeuvre the horrible brute.
> But are you sure that what was said,
> you know, is unsaid now. Do you really hate him?

IRA

Why ask? My feelings have been maimed.
In twelve months, so much has happened,
so much of which I feel ashamed,
because of my love for him.

(*As she speaks,* EBERHARD *lets her hair fall down.*)

                        I've humbled myself.
My unconditional surrender
has brought me Vittorio's throttled look of hatred,
or, sometimes, when his mood was tender,
impersonal contempt, neutral disbelief, boredom,
as if I were a naked thing,
a stained mattress, say, not flesh with needs,
the need to open and to cling.

EBERHARD

(*Rapidly repairing her hair style*)
Get rid of Vittorio, take on Orestes, sit still.

IRA

Don't be so free with your advice.
It isn't that simple. I don't act on strategic lines.
My thoughts are like a set of dice,
changing all the time. Shaken by events.
I'm way beyond the rational stage.
I can't keep up a poker face. It isn't me.
What I need to act is – rage.

EBERHARD

But what more provocation could you want?
He loves a public enemy
and he makes no secret of it. He's flagrant about
Annette LeSkye's hegemony.

IRA

Thank you. Thank you very much. Sometimes,
   Eberhard,
I think you want to drive me mad.
I'm a woman, remember? With feelings.
With nerves. I'm not an ironclad.
So stop treating me like the SS *Princess Ira*.
You're right. We can go. Nothing to keep us.
Except the ghost of sentiment:
a girl who would like to be loved, for whom
this shame is no impediment.
She won't go away. She hangs on, whispering:
perhaps Vittorio will change,
look up, lost in thought, see me there, and smile
so naturally, it won't seem strange.
(*Grimaces.*)
No, it won't seem strange. It'll seem impossible.
He only wants to hurt me now.
Let's pay him back. Let's be obstructive. He'd like
me gone, but why should I kotow
when I can spoil things for them so effectively
just by staying on in Rome?
My loss of face will be magnified if
it looks as though I daren't go home.
The sympathy, my dear. Germans will demand
the mother's death, not just the son's.
You wouldn't believe how much I want to get her.

EBERHARD

Her temperament is like a nun's:
naturally chaste, dedicated to a single end,
and you're mistaken if you think
she derives any pleasure from depriving you
of Tarzan and his jungle stink.
If she liked his mating calls, you might (mightn't you?)
expect some signs of happiness,
not that same drab look which so perfectly matches
her wardrobe's one and only dress.

IRA

Her coldness is why the king is kept on heat.
And his ambition is to steep
himself in the subject, saturate himself in details,
till he can *do it* in his sleep.
Imagination. It always outstrips the truth.
The naked body offers less
in the way of breathtaking beauty than
it does of ordinariness.
We're all the same. When his hands take off her clothes,
and not his mind, he'll be surprised
to learn her unique flesh is any body's:
familiar, strange, as advertised.
Then she'll suffer, like me, for holding nothing back.
We are only women. Yes,

the secret of the body is there is no secret.
We have no secret of success.
Only this. Avoid failure. Hence Vittorio,
the aptly named. His victories
eclipsed his father's reputation: not
one English town he didn't seize.
London was left without a single landmark.
And if you like those kind of looks,
handsome. Not a chiselled effeminate face.
Rugged. I was on tenterhooks
till he proposed. I should have turned him down.
And now I will. Orestes is
the better man. His virtues make up for
the lack of Mussolini fizz.

EBERHARD
Odd you should mention him.

(IRA *quickly turns. As she goes to meet* ORESTES, EBERHARD *addresses the ether.*)

Hello, Klaus.

Scene 2

Throughout this scene, ORESTES *plays nervously with a penknife, throwing it from hand to hand, taking it in and out of his pocket.*

IRA
The noble Count! What brings you here?
Business? Or the pleasure of seeing an old flame?
Sentiment, or your career?

ORESTES

Your alternatives aren't incompatible,
but do you really need to ask?
You must be able to see that underneath
this formal bureaucratic mask
there are third-degree burns like a Kokoschka oil.
I am the moth. You are the furnace.
Smell the burning? Why do we go on thinking
that only hot things ever burn us?
I suppose your feelings are cold as ever?
I won't be cold until I'm dead.
Not before. I tried the Russian front, half hoping
for a bullet in the head
which would take my mind off you. Stalingrad was just
a shot at getting shot of you,
as far as I was concerned. But they always killed
another member of my crew.
And I am spared to stand here hale,
if hardly hearty. How I manage to be flippant,
I'm not quite sure. This is the end.
No further. Not a step. Unless you love me.
Which thing you don't. So why pretend?
Shall I shoot myself? Take an overdose?
Refuse the future, send it back?
Dear God, I no longer wish to subscribe to Life.
Things are looking far too black.
I'm serious. I make you sick. You make me feel ill.
Ill enough to want to die.

IRA

(*Flustered by his facetious tone*)
It's clear there are, as your answer makes clear,
a few things we should clarify.
Your duties. You are the Führer's delegate,

his trusted envoy to the king.
You bear our ultimatum: give up the boy,
or hear the high explosive whistling
through its teeth, as Rome appears and disappears,
eidetic in the riven dark.
Trinitrotoluene will start the holocaust.
It doesn't need your personal spark.
Private affairs, Klaus, are none of this affair.
My question was rhetorical
earlier, nervous chit-chat. Forgive me.

ORESTES

Of course. You are the oracle.
But I'm not without my own news either.
Vittorio has turned us down.
A flat refusal, for whatever reason.
Therefore, I don't deserve that frown:
my duty done, I can please myself, displease
myself, exactly as I choose.
Only my future rests on your decision.

IRA

Amazing that he chose the Jews.

ORESTES

God? Or Vittorio? I see I have your full attention.
I sense your answer will be 'no'.

IRA

Why exaggerate my so-called indifference?
My passion for Vittorio
wasn't uninfluenced by my sense of duty.

The Führer ordered. I complied.
And the contract was drawn up by lawyers.
Which meant you were disqualified,
but he'll bear witness, won't you, Eberhard?
I've sometimes sobbed for you for days.

(*They both look at* EBERHARD, *who returns their stare.*)

ORESTES

And in your weaker moments wept for weeks,
until distress defaced your face,
and all your loveliness was lost, don't tell me.
For me? You didn't give a rap:
you used me like a table napkin, not a lover.
I spent an hour in your lap.
You pressed me to your lips twice before you
 dropped me.

IRA

Know thyself, said Socrates.
Easy. All my life, I'd known nothing else,
and what I wanted was release
from the thought of being me. Little me.
Like someone living in one room
without a change of clean clothes, I stank
of me. I'd lie there, reading doom
in the dull wallpaper like re-reading an old
 newspaper.
I'm very grateful to you still
for finding me, all my faded life, exciting.
And hurting you . . .

ORESTES
> you felt a thrill.

You were sick of yourself. Now you could be sick of me.

IRA
Oh, Klaus, I owe you everything.

ORESTES
But I can't cash in gratitude for love.
And nor can you. You love the king.
You dislike him, but you have to have him, like a drug.
If only I were your addiction.

IRA
No. I'd need you, but in my guts I'd hate your guts.

ORESTES
I disagree with your prediction.
Now I'm like a dose of medicine. Better for you,
but all the same I make you retch.
He makes you come, for a short time, to your senses,
but after that you start to lech
and what excited your disgust a minute since
incites desire, its opposite.
I want you helpless in my arms like that,
slavish in your appetite.
He hates you. Get rid of him. The perfect opportunity.

IRA
The perfect nothing of the kind. Who told you that now his appetite is dull?

Do I look like something on the side of his plate?
Unappetizing, pitiful?

ORESTES

Ira, no one ever believed that stuff about
the one room and the tawdry self,
except for you. You've always been a princess,
and not some spinster on the shelf.
You're a great beauty. Anyway, why ask me?
Why *me*? With all this vehemence?
Five years of solid devotion says I never said
that your attractions weren't immense.
Ira, it wasn't me. Not guilty. Try Vittorio.

IRA

Klaus, telephone the Führer now.
Tell him he can bomb the whole of Italy flat.
I want to see that bastard's brow
crammed in the dirt. Say that to the Führer.
I sound as if I love the man?

ORESTES

Yes. In a way, you do. Come back to Germany.
Wasn't that the Führer's plan
if Vittorio turned out to be recalcitrant?
Stay, and you're a hostage here,
a liability. Leave all this behind,
and then your hatred will be clear.
Be beautiful, be broken in Berlin:
break every heart in unison.

IRA

I should agree, but suppose he marries her,
his alibi that I had gone?

I might be held responsible, made a scapegoat,
if he took a Jewish wife.

ORESTES

Ah-ha, passion's brilliant special pleading.
The best-equipped Swiss army knife
isn't more versatile, resourceful, ingenious.
The heart has reasons, Pascal said,
of which reason knows nothing. And he was right.
When the heart controls the head . . .

IRA

Talking to you is like talking to a psychoanalyst.
For God's sake, put that bloody knife
back in your pocket before I stab you. I've been
a loyal German all my life
and that's how I intend to carry on. Service:
to me the word means everything.
I'm not a free agent. My hidden motives,
whether I hate or love the king,
are irrelevant. The Führer sent me here.
And here I stay unless recalled
or dismissed. Tell him to choose. Me or the boy.
The Fatherland has been stonewalled
long enough. No compromise. One or the other.
If it's the boy, then I go back
if Vittorio is prepared to grant permission.

(*Exit* IRA, *followed by* EBERHARD.)

Scene 3

ORESTES *alone*.

ORESTES
Permission! Do cows moo, ducks quack,
dogs bark? Is Hegel's dialectic boring?
Are dictators autocratic?
I don't anticipate endless paperwork.
Permission will be automatic.
A rubber stamp. Probably with the sole of his boot.
He's only looking for a pretext
to prise her loose and get his grips on Annette
  LeSkye.
That's why his face looks so perplexed:
his mind can only manage one thing at a time.
So all I need to do is ask,
then we'll chat about our different views of Ira,
at length, in terms of parallax,
with reference to Einstein's general theory.
He'll have a lot to contribute.

Scene 4

Enter VITTORIO *and* FENICE *to* ORESTES.

VITTORIO
Good. Excellent. Fenice, his excellency. Orestes.
Well met. Our ridiculous dispute
before. I was just looking for you to say
that, well, I take back everything.
I can't think what I was thinking about.
The slightest sign of bullying,
not that I'd dream of accusing anyone of anything,

but you know how it is, the stress
of confrontation, things regrettably get out of hand,
and so . . . Where was I now? Yes. Yes,
all things considered, I can see that Axis interests
are paramount. Back goes the boy.
Or, rather, *on* to Germany, as the Führer demands.

ORESTES

Good news. From Naples to Savoy,
the people will marvel at your diplomatic thrift,
the way you have avoided strife
and purchased peace so cheaply:
the cost of only one small life.

VITTORIO

I haven't finished, Count. The alliance needs
more ballast, so I undertake
to marry Ira without further delay –
a union you'll appreciate,
I know, because the concord of our countries
is something dear to your heart,
and I know you've been distressed to see
two such firm allies drift apart.
Tomorrow you can give her away. Today,
please tell her what we have in mind.

ORESTES

(*Aside*)
    Knowing your dirty mind, sperm on her entrails.

(*Exit* ORESTES.)

Scene 5

VITTORIO

Fenice, if I say I find
that count a bit of a cunt, is that unreasonable?
I feel refreshed, as if I'd slept
for sixteen hours solid, all by myself.
I can't believe I ever wept
over that woman. Over any woman, come to that.
Vittorio is back on form:
blood pressure, bowels, back to normal. Pulse rate
steady as a metronome.

FENICE

You look champion. Like barley-fed beef.
As handsome as your photograph.
Winning the battle of the sexes isn't easy.
You've got to be a chief of staff.
I couldn't see why you were taking orders,
behaving like a raw recruit.

VITTORIO

Worse. Dismissed with ignominy, broken,
measured for a demob suit.
Well, now she gets her marching orders.
The bitch can goose step all the way
to Germany. When I think of the risk I was taking,
the price I was prepared to pay:
a third world war . . .

FENICE
    . . . Goebbels on the radio . . .

VITTORIO
. . . to feel, just once, that long, long look,
searching for the father somewhere in the son.
Platonic love!

FENICE
It makes me puke.
But you bounced back again all right, thank
 goodness.
It's your elastic temperament.

VITTORIO
Just don't stretch it too far, Fenice. Or else
it might snap back by accident,
you never know, and wipe that face off your smile.

FENICE
It suits you when you're passionate.
No wonder women can't resist your majesty.

VITTORIO
With one exception. I can't wait
to see her snivelling beside her luggage.
You'd think maternal feeling would
have persuaded her to save the kid, eh?
There's some ingredient in their blood,
a female hormone or something, isn't there?
I was certain she'd relent.
But it could have been goodbye at boarding school.
A fixed demeanour like cement.
Stiff upper lip and upper class. Very English.
A hug, a stare, a little speech:
'Always remember, Angus, whose son you are.'
Poor little blighter. What a bitch.
She's in no position to refuse my offer.

FENICE
You shouldn't let her rattle you.

VITTORIO
You're right. I've got the whip hand. Not her.
So why should I be in a stew
while Lady Muck serves herself up like iced tea?
Shit, she's so bloody arrogant,
so sure of her breeding, her classic looks, as if
she were a rare, endangered plant
in a world of fucking turnips. Christ almighty.
Sometimes, I swear she makes me feel
sub-human. Eager, panting,
bewildered, bound to come to heel.
With so much power, she doesn't need a plan.
She's sure she'll get me on my knees.
But I'll have her naked on all fours
before we're through and saying please
and thank you for the privilege of licking clean
the welted edges of my shoes.

FENICE
And why not? That should bring her down to earth.
Who is she to pick and choose?
Ira's much more your sort, a proper woman,
the type who likes a chap with testes,
with a bit of energy, of get it up and go, eh?
Instead of trusting to Orestes,
mind, I think you should propose to her yourself.

VITTORIO
Agreed. That's excellent advice.
But first, one more visit to the widow.
You've left out one essential spice
in your recipe for my happiness:

the torment of Annette LeSkye.
Don't worry. I don't want much. Hardly anything.
I only want to watch her cry.
As a scientific experiment.
To see the surface tension build
to breaking point, glitter and go out.
(*His own voice suddenly, vestigially uncertain*)
As if the last of light was spilled
and there would never ever be any more again.

FENICE

Go. Go. You're still in love with her.
You're a bloody fool. Listen to yourself.
A fool. Excuse, forgive me, sir.
(*A dangerous moment, defused by* FENICE's *sincerity*.)
I care about you as if you were my own lad.

VITTORIO

I know you want what's best for me,
Fenice. So don't be scared. It's all right.
You promised Dad you'd always see
me safe. Across the river, into the trees, eh?
I know. I know. You always have.
What am I going to do, Fenice?
I don't like this. I'm like her slave.

FENICE

The trouble is you've gone public. Told the world.
We can't go back. We must go on.

VITTORIO

Stick to plan like sticking to a live cable.
Take Ira on and drop the son.
Her son. If I stabbed her with this bowie knife
and felt her flesh resist, then give,

with the sigh of a whetstone,
I couldn't kill what makes her live
more effectively than by giving up that boy.
I *can't*. I kill her in my mind
like this – and invent a vein, blue beside the knife
   point.
I'd give her anything, be kind,
care for the boy, if only she would care for me.
I'm dog shit, dog shit on her shoe.
A smell in her head she wants to be rid of.
Good. Fine. The plan. I'll see it through.

ACT THREE

Scene 1

Usual changing of the guard. Lights up on ORESTES *and* OLDENBURG. ORESTES *has his back to the audience. He is quite still, then his head gives a pronounced twitch and he begins to laugh. An ordinary laugh – but unprovoked and very long. Approximately thirty seconds, or until the audience feels uncomfortable – and then a bit more.*

ORESTES

(*Turns, his face a mask of tears.*)
You have to laugh. In a few years, we'll laugh at this.

OLDENBURG

Please get a grip on yourself, Klaus.
Steady now. This doesn't help anything, you know.
The situation calls for *nous*
not hysteria. Hysteria's the last thing we need.

ORESTES

Who says that we need your advice,
if it comes to that? You're like a stockbroker
arranging me a selling price
for a few stocks and shares, a little nest egg,
a windfall, an inheritance.
Your reasonable voice carefully pointing out
the risks, the element of chance.
Don't you understand anything? I've lost everything.
The lot. It's gone. There's nothing left.
But I'm not going to let them treat me like this.
There's only one solution: theft.
I'm not going to go without. I'm going to steal Ira.

OLDENBURG

All right, abduct her then. But please,
please keep your voice down. Right down.
Remember where you are. Appease
the household gods. There are guards everywhere.
At night, you hear the palace tick
with their footsteps like a time bomb.
Come on. Here, wipe your eyes. Quick,
before anyone sees the state you're in.
That's good. This place is dangerous.
Listen. You can hear the silence listening.
Anything strange a stranger does,
like going mad, tends to be noticed,
and reported straightaway.
Why did you even look for Ira, looking like this?

ORESTES

Why? State of total disarray.
I don't know. I didn't think what I was doing.
Shock. I was in a state of shock.
Maybe I was going to threaten them both.
Insult her and her butcher's block.

OLDENBURG

What would that have achieved? What was the point?

ORESTES

My head felt tight, that's all. Too tight.
And I had to get out somehow. Too many thoughts.
So that I couldn't think. That's right:
Ira's wedding to Vittorio was in the way.
It's difficult. I can't explain,
but I was next to myself. Yes? Watching Orestes
as if Orestes was insane.
And I felt sorry. I felt sorry for myself.

Except my hands. They frightened me.
I recognized them, but they weren't mine any more.
They were just hands. Completely free.
And they wanted to burst Vittorio's eyes.

OLDENBURG

Perhaps you should stop blaming him?
Perhaps Vittorio's tortured in his own way?

ORESTES

The odds on that are pretty slim.
You're wrong. My misery is what motivates him.
Yes. Otherwise, he'd let her go.
He doesn't love Ira. He savours my suffering,
a gourmet relishing each throe,
each pitiful spasm. Why else snatch her back
when he was rid of her at last?
She was falling in love with me again, talking
tenderly about the past.
Ready to go back. One word was all she wanted.
One final 'no' and she would leave.

OLDENBURG

And settle down with you somewhere in Germany?
I can't believe that you believe . . .

ORESTES

I heard her raging about Vittorio.
I saw saliva whiten, here,
and here, at the corners of her mouth.

OLDENBURG

(*Pauses, then very drily*)
Like crumbs of brewer's yeast in beer,
I dare say. So what? What does that prove? Nothing.

How can you see a thing like that
and not see that Vittorio is her disease?
He's poisoned her like paraquat.
He's gone deep, eaten into her very bones.
It's fatal. What you saw was fever.
Delirium. Don't trust her. Don't abduct her.
Don't even say goodbye. Just leave her.
Whatever you do, don't force her to go now.
Don't. Every second of your life
together, she'd loathe and despise you because
she's yours and not Vittorio's wife.
You can forget about flesh. She'll laugh when you
    come.

ORESTES

It isn't love I want, it's fear.
Could abduction have any other outcome?
Soon she won't have any strength to sneer.
I'll teach her to cringe every time I move.
She'll learn about unhappiness.
Women bruise easily. I'll leave my fingerprints.
She'll never wear a sleeveless dress.
I'm deep. I'll drown her in my sorrows.
I'll drag her down, and keep her there.

OLDENBURG

And your good name dragged down, too, Klaus.
It's kidnap, not *chemin de fer*.

ORESTES

I'll take the gamble either way. I think
I must be clinically depressed,
don't you? I mean, the boy should mean something.
This diplomat is unimpressed
by his own diplomacy, however.

I try to fail, but I succeed –
and therefore I fail. This is ironic.
My moral sense has atrophied
in a world where omnipresent irony is God.
Why should we bother to be good?
Take a close look. The hands of any head of state
in recent times are brown with blood.
The Führer not excepted. Ask any Jew or gypsy.
So what? A real murderer
like Churchill dies inhaling vomit after
drinking Louis Roederer
champagne all night with Brendan Bracken.
Dies in his sleep quite peacefully.
There is no justice working in the universe.
No other God but irony.
Abduction or duty? It doesn't matter which.
It all gets shitty in the end.
If life is punishment, let's commit a crime.
But you, you've been a loyal friend
to me. Thank you. I love you and leave you
with one last charge to carry out:
take Angus LeSkye back to the Fatherland.
You'll get on then, without a doubt.

OLDENBURG

Government receptions, speeches, spurious
acclaim, the Iron Cross first class,
heels clicking like a typing pool, Himmler twinkling
approval through that rimless glass:
I don't think I could bear that, Klaus, thanks all the
    same.
A friend in need is a friend indeed.
When I was little that expression bothered me.
I wondered if the one in need

was the one who needed help or the friend who
   helped.
I'd spend all day just working out
the different possible permutations.
I was a queer kid. Strange, stout,
lonely, nervous. I'll help you kidnap Ira.
You get your men all worked up, make
sure that the sub is action-stations ready.
It'll be a piece of cake.

        ORESTES
Schwarzwälder Kirschtorte.

        OLDENBURG
        Mit Sahne.
And there's a tunnel to the quay
hidden in the foundations. I'll show you where.

        ORESTES
(*Punches* OLDENBURG's *arm.*)
Tonight's the night.

        OLDENBURG
        We're on a spree.

(*Pause because neither of them knows quite what to do with the sudden exhilaration.*)

But until then you must control your emotions.
Be circumspect, or else we're lost.

        ORESTES
Don't worry. I'll be formal as a calling card:
ambassadorial, embossed,
hand-engraved, the highest grade of board.

You're a good man. I'll pay you back.

OLDENBURG
Here comes Ira. Smile please, Klaus. Don't overdo it.
Try to forget you're on the rack.

Scene 2

Enter IRA *and* EBERHARD.

ORESTES
Germany joins Italy in holy matrimony:
Vittorio is yours again.

IRA
So I've been given to understand – and that you
were looking for me to explain.

ORESTES
I take it you accept the king's proposal?

IRA
Why not confess I'm gratified,
after so many months of faithlessness,
to find he wants me at his side
just as I was preparing to leave for good?
Yet even so, I don't pretend
he isn't moved as much by state policy
as love. His passion is a blend,
unlike yours, of the public with the private.

ORESTES
I must protest, defend the king –
and so defend your great beauty's reputation.
Your eyes could tie a knot in string.
To bind a mere lover hand and foot is child's play
by comparison. You're pleased?

IRA
The marriage was arranged. The inevitable
is better recognized and seized
than resisted fruitlessly. I'll do my duty.
A princess can't be set on love.
Obedience outweighs personal preference.
And yet, if push had come to shove . . .
well, you saw just how close I came to leaving.

ORESTES
Can I suggest we stop this game?
You know our hearts are anarchists, not flunkeys.
They serve themselves. You're not to blame
for what I'm going through. Love is selfish.
Yours. Mine. Therefore, I can't complain.
If you can't please me and please yourself,
why should you go against the grain?
With your permission, this sad interview should
   end.

Scene 3

IRA *and* EBERHARD *are left alone after the exit of* ORESTES *and* OLDENBURG.

IRA
What unpredictable restraint.

EBERHARD
The tighter the shoe, the bigger the bunion,
the tightest stays, the fastest faint,
they used to say when I was a young girl.
(*Puts on Lancashire accent.*)
Poor chap, he looked well below par:
fed up, eaten up, stirred up and bottled up,
ugh, like a tapeworm in a jar.
He used to have a good colour before.
(*Normal voice.*)
It's not all that surprising, though,
is it? Considering how he's scuppered himself
by being here. Twelve months ago,
you were engaged. Like a taxi. And kept waiting.
But now he takes you for a ride
to dodge Orestes and the German ultimatum.

IRA
You think the king is terrified?
Of what? Germany's economic miracle?
The currency in cigarettes?
Food coupons? Clothes coupons? Petrol coupons?
Our powdered egg? Our foreign debts?
The haemorrhage on the Russian front? Forget it.
We can't afford another war.
And anyhow, Vittorio would probably win.
It's difficult to keep the score
of all his exploits in the field of battle.
His prowess in another place
depends less on words than on the mouth itself.
The way it locks on to your face
for what can begin to seem for ever:
you feel the rhythm of the jaws
working, eating your head like a cantaloup,
efficiently, without a pause.

And his fingers are very long and curious.

EBERHARD
Perhaps you should contain yourself . . .
(*Scots accent.*)
Brazen hizzie, haud your blether. Lady Och Aye.

IRA
Oh no. Let's leave. No time for stealth.
I want to luxuriate, not waste time on her.

Scene 4

IRA *and* EBERHARD *are leaving when* ANNETTE'S *voice detains them with its natural authority when it is raised.*

ANNETTE
I promise not to keep you long
but I must speak to your royal highness now.
Their obligations to the strong
are constantly present to the weak,
but power has its duties, too.
Noblesse oblige.

IRA
A precept of my English nanny's,
bless her. But I'm obliged to you
for the reminder.

ANNETTE
I don't want to antagonize
your royal highness. That would serve
no purpose at all. Please don't misconstrue
straightforwardness as brazen nerve.

You have everything. You want for nothing.
I have nothing but the task
of saving my son. I'm desperate. Forgive me.
I ask because I have to ask.
I have no husband. I have only a son.
You'll marry soon and have a child.
Then you'll feel what I feel, what all mothers feel.
We're not quite civilized. We're wild,
instinct with instincts. I'd take out this breast now
to still a baby's tracking face.
Bad taste? Buttons. The kneading mouth of need itself
undoes this dress. I rest my case
here in my hand. I have felt the milk moving
through this breast like something homesick
for a destination. My son is a small boy.
Perhaps Vittorio would pick
some colony, sentence us to exile there,
if only you would intercede.
Help us. Please.

IRA
      If I could, I would. But I can't.
I have to take the Führer's lead
in this, as in everything. Vittorio is independent.
Ask him yourself. When he has weighed
the argument you've just produced so tellingly,
the king could easily be swayed.

(*Exit* IRA *and* EBERHARD.)

Scene 5

ANNETTE *and* KATE.

ANNETTE
She *snubs* a plea for mercy?
(*Nods slowly.*)
       And demeans herself.

KATE
Speak to the king. Her little quip,
whatever she intended, isn't such bad advice.
He'll listen to your ladyship.

ANNETTE
Unless I tell the king what he wants to hear,
he's deaf, or else he's violent.
Kate, I've said goodbye to Angus already.
And come to terms with what that meant.
It's all over. I'm worn out. I could sleep nearly.

KATE
Well, God forgive your ladyship,
because I won't. Look. Use everything in your power.
And don't you dare let this chance slip.

Scene 6

Enter VITTORIO *and* FENICE *to* ANNETTE *and* KATE.

VITTORIO
I thought you said Ira was here, Fenice.

FENICE
I thought she was.

ANNETTE
       A snub. Again.
My very presence is an affront, my grief
a social gaffe. That much is plain.

VITTORIO
What's she going on about?

FENICE
              Just ignore her.

VITTORIO
(*To* ANNETTE)
   What's all this rhubarb? Insolence.
Whispering. You curtsy when you see me, madam.
Curtsy. If you've got any sense
of self-preservation, you'll remember that.
Fenice, let's pack off the brat.
Has that sealed compartment been coupled up?

FENICE
(*Takes out his watch.*)
It has by now.

ANNETTE
(*Goaded, but cool*)
          The thermostat,
or whatever it is that controls our relationship,
is fixed too close to boiling point.
Can't we lower the temperature and talk?
Your self-esteem is out of joint
because of something I said carelessly, isn't it?

Forgive me. And forgive my son.
You were offering me your friendship not long ago.

VITTORIO
It's too late now. What's done is done.

ANNETTE
You said you'd see Rome itself undone for me.
You said you'd rewrite history.

VITTORIO
As you do now. The pledge was conditional.
Think back and search your memory.
Go over every word. There *was* something, wasn't
 there?
I wanted something in return.
But now I don't want anything at all from you.
For all I care, the boy can burn.
I promised you everything. For what? A promise.
A promise that you wouldn't give.
Christ, you wouldn't even concede the possibility
that I was human, fit to live.

ANNETTE
You of all people should understand pride,
ingrained, patrician sense of caste.
I have never asked for anything in all my life.
Requests were orders in the past.
Always. Even though I seemed to ask, I ordered.
I'm humbled now. I say please. Please.
And now I mean it. Look, look, because of you,
I go down on my hands and knees.

VITTORIO
Get off me. Get up. Now. No. You hate me.

You couldn't bear to be in debt
to anyone – but me least of all, least of all.
Even your son's reprieve, I bet,
you'd loathe it if it came from me.
But I propose to spare you that.
I wouldn't want you to feel obligated.

ANNETTE
Your mistress is no diplomat,
try as she may. Come on, Kate. Let's go.

KATE
I won't.

ANNETTE
What else is there to add?
A deposition? A recital of my wrongs?
Kate, what would only make us sad,
he knows already. He brought it all about.
I am reduced, as you can see,
in every circumstance. Pomp and circumstance.
A phrase. *Othello*. Elgar. Me.
Slowly shrinking into insignificance.
I saw my father's fatal stroke.
Relatives were led out to the kitchen garden.
In the rain. I saw the soldiers soak
the walls and the rugs and the books in petrol.
And things evaporation blurred.
Then they threw in a lighted lighter. It purred.
Going through the air it purred
and then the whole house gasped like a gas oven.
With Hector dead, the boy survived,
and we found ourselves alive in Italy
and glad to be here. We contrived
to feel secure, to think things would get better.
How? I could feel you could be kind,

that this palace wasn't meant to be a prison,
that there was something else behind
every show of anger. Always. Something tender.
Something. But clearly, I was wrong.
You aren't the generous man I took you for.

VITTORIO

(*To* FENICE)
Well, you can go. I won't be long.

(*Exit* FENICE.)

Only want to say you can still save little Angus.
Not that there's all that much to save:
fifteen freckles and one metre what? of skin.
Situation's pretty grave,
but not absolutely beyond salvaging.
I know I sound a total sham.
Why in the name of God am I talking like this?
Heroic as a telegram,
like something out of *Boy's Own* or *British Bulldog*?
I want to tell your ladyship.
What I want to say is that I still want you.
Your hands. That English upper lip.
The way you have of holding your head.
I need it all. I won't let go.
Don't make me hate you any more. Think of Angus.
The boy should be allowed to grow.
You could watch his frame fill out. His voice break.
You'll recognize the way he starts
to stand exactly like his father,
and then the way his mouth half parts
and his wrist cocks, just so, to see his watch.
Things only you can know about.
Things you'll never know about unless you marry me.

For you I'm quite prepared to flout
my promise to Ira, Germany, everything.
Provided everything is sure
between us. Decide. Once and for all. Decide
as I've decided: kill or cure.
Take Ira's place or take the consequences –
for you and little Angus both.

(*Exit* VITTORIO.)

KATE

What did I say? Didn't I tell your ladyship?
I *knew*. I would have sworn an oath.

ANNETTE

I took your advice. To what purpose? The choice leaves
no choice. I must condemn my son.

KATE

My lady, you're over-scrupulous. All things,
even mourning, have their season.
Be shrewd. Your husband was. Given these two evils,
he'd choose the lesser of the two.

ANNETTE

After Hector, Vittorio is unthinkable.

KATE

So what is thinkable to you?
The Gestapo don't play games with anyone.
Except perhaps the odd small boy.
For God's sake, exercise your imagination.
They do. Or things begin to cloy.
They like to make death diverting for themselves.
There's dying first before there's death.

ANNETTE

Don't you ever dare lecture me about dying.
I've seen it close to, smelt its breath.
Hector's tongue was black between his teeth
when they cut his body down.
We were made to wait for a war photographer.
He lay there, looking old, a frown
on his face. And then his jaw fell wide open
and all his dusty face relaxed.
He was unrecognizable with this grey dust.
The ends of his moustache were waxed
and under all the filth still kept two fine points
when nothing else could keep its shape.
They urinated over his face and used a gun
to prop the chin and close the gape
when they finally took their photographs.
My husband's body was defiled.
They defiled it. And you want me to marry
the man responsible. He smiled,
took nips from a hip flask, shouted orders,
the palace burning in each eye.
Quite handsome. He ran his hands through his hair
and posed for photographs. I die
when I remember how confident he looked.
Animated, vital, quick.
I couldn't let him touch me with those hands.
Touching my mouth. I would be sick.
Don't ask me to defile myself and Hector.
For what? A little extra life.
It would be life degraded to existence.
That animal. I'm Hector's wife.

KATE

Yes. And you're Angus's mother. Hector's dead.
The boy's alive.

ANNETTE
What can I do?
You're right, Kate. I'm wrong, wrong, wrong.
I must do what he asked me to
when he kissed me goodbye and took Angus in his arms.
He looked at me, without a word,
without even a smile, and gave his son back to me.
He didn't need to speak. I heard
the sense. This is my body. This is my blood.
It wasn't even blasphemy.
It was God's own truth. Words put into his mouth.
If I ask him, he'll advise me
what I should do now.

KATE
My lady? Hector's dead.

ANNETTE
I feel as if he's still alive,
as if he's there but I can't quite see him.
We die but somehow we survive.
I don't mean really. That isn't how it works.
I need to think what he would say,
so I have to imagine him first, listening.
His head is bent. He looks away.
I can see his hands, too, listening on his knees,
so intent they never move.
Glistening tufts of ginger hair. His signet ring.
And then the letters on the ring.
Until he looks up at me and interrupts.
And tells me what to tell the king.

ACT FOUR

Scene 1

No passo romano. *One guard is visible right at the back of the stage, but does not move.* ANNETTE LESKYE *and* KATE *are sewing together in silence. Hold it. Then* KATE *bursts into tears and is unable to speak for a time.*

KATE

Sorry. I really don't know why I keep doing this.
Because I'm so relieved perhaps.
Now everything's fixed at last I seem to need
the odd hysterical collapse
(that's all it is) to, you know, ease all that tension.

ANNETTE

You're shaking like a carburettor.

KATE

Finished. All over. No more fuss. Blow my nose.
Don't worry. It's nothing. I'm better.
Your ladyship was right to think
what Hector would have said if he'd been alive.
On our own, we reached the brink
of complete disaster. Angus was nearly gone.
But now the little man's OK.
We. You've got Vittorio's sworn pledge for that.
You heard him give it straightaway,
as soon as you spoke. He was only waiting.
Now he'll do anything for you.
I'm quite sure he really loves you, my lady.
The man is waiting for a cue
to act generously. His throne, his people,
are yours if you will – only speak

to him less coldly, a little more tenderly.
Like everyone who loves, he's weak,
in spite of the power he has. Under the façade,
he's like an anxious invalid
who worries about everyone else's health.
The boy: look how he's cosseted
our Angus with his personal bodyguard
in case those Germans try some trick:
a bit of body-snatching, or a murder.
The king's own guard. It's ten ranks thick.
I counted. You can hardly see little Angus.

ANNETTE

But all the same I have to see
Angus now, before I go to the basilica.
(*Sardonically echoes* KATE's *'little Angus'*.)
Just little him, and little me.

KATE

Why not wait till after the ceremony?
Then you can see him when you like,
your access unrestricted by any German threat.
They will return to Hitler's Reich
and everything will return to normal. Better:
your captive son will be a prince,
royal, as Vittorio's heir by adoption.

ANNETTE

Now, Kate. Let's see the boy now, since
this will be the last time we'll see each other.

KATE

I knew there must be something more.
Too calm. You were . . . How could you sit there
    sewing?

ANNETTE

I've told you everything before,
always, and I won't keep back anything now.
I know you love me, Kate.

KATE

O God.

ANNETTE

But I thought you knew me better than that.
You think I'd touch that filthy clod,
or let his fingers finger me at their leisure?
He'd have to force his tongue in here
and, raw as it was, I'd bite it clean through.
Oh yes, I'd grit my teeth and shear
till it came off in my mouth. Red as a dog's thing.
How could you think that I'd accept
Vittorio after Hector? I thought you'd know.

KATE

My body knew. My body wept.

ANNETTE

To save Angus I'll go through with the marriage.
I've thought it out. This is the plan:
a great deal will depend on your discretion
and on how well I know my man.
I believe Vittorio can be honourable,
so if I marry him, he'll stick
to the bargain and protect Angus as agreed.
But, *but*, he mustn't see the trick
I play to save my honour with my son's life.
I've planned a careful suicide:
after the wedding, before his conjugal rights.

KATE
How?

ANNETTE
A window opened far too wide.
Nothing dramatic. No guns. No daggers. Just a fall.
A tragic accident. I'll lean
against the drawn curtains as I talk to him.
I'll show you, Kate, the room I mean.
It's high. I'll have a drink in my hand. Friendly.
He'll never hear the sentence end.
I won't scream. I'll look a bit surprised, that's all.
And then you play your part, my friend.

KATE
Iron. What do you want me to do, my lady?

ANNETTE
He must be favourably disposed
towards Angus, encouraged, not allowed to lapse.
You'll speak for me. You'll be my ghost.
You'll tell Vittorio that I told you I loved him.
With circumstantial details, please.
So surprised, you remember everything exactly:
how you were here on your knees,
lowering the hem of my silk wedding dress.
And how your mouth was full of pins
and you pricked yourself when I said I loved him.
Blood in your mouth. I saw you wince
and I was cross with you for pulling faces.
You think you can remember that?
Good. Now Angus. Never tell the boy the truth.
No. No heroics. Keep it flat.
Flat and even perfunctory. He can respect me,
but he must love Vittorio

because that's the one way he's sure to survive.
His father, Hector, told me so.
And so clearly, Kate. So. So. So. So. I could see so.
And hear. I mustn't break down now.
Make sure the king and Angus love each other.
They must. It doesn't matter how.
Don't cry. Here comes Ira. Borrow my handkerchief.

(*Exit* ANNETTE *and* KATE.)

Scene 2

EBERHARD *and* IRA.

EBERHARD
You minded, though, that time he used
her Christian name accidentally. Didn't you?
From one 'Annette' you soon deduced
a whole catalogue of furtive fornications
between them. You could smell her on
his fingers, you said. O, and other places.
You knew exactly what they'd done.
You broke all your fingernails on him
and then yourself. Your cheeks were scratched
till they bled. And now? Nothing. Not a murmur.
Maybe you think you weren't well matched
and they're the ideal couple and wish them well?
They're getting married. Do you hear?
It's not jealous paranoia. It's on the wireless.
Poor lass, they've broadcast your worst fear.

IRA
Did you send for Orestes, as I asked you?

EBERHARD

He's on his way. Look now. He's here.
Ira, princess, he only wants to look after you,
and if you let him just be near
you, he's grateful. And he's loyal like me,
through thick and thin.

(*Enter* ORESTES, *exhilarated, despite his sense of* IRA'*s depression. For him, ebullient.*)

Scene 3

ORESTES
           Can it be true?
For once I am wanted. Not an imposition.
You ask for me. I come to you.
So simple. I can't tell you how right it feels.
Forget this wrong you can't forgive.
I thought you'd look unhappy, Ira, but not
as if you hadn't long to live,
as if life itself was turning your stomach,
sick to death behind your thin façade.
You mustn't let Vittorio see how he's hurt you.
Clench your teeth and swallow hard.

IRA
I want to know if you're still in love with me.

ORESTES
Give me your hand. Good. Put it here
on my heart. Here. Can you feel the systole?
It's like a telephone, my dear.
Ringing for you. Only you can answer it.
Everything I've ever said,

praise, slanders, insults, lies, tenderness,
and all I've done, the way I fled
and returned, this inflammation of the eyes,
is nothing but a telephone
ringing and ringing and ringing and ringing.
Until you answer, I'm alone.

IRA

This great love, prove it. Do something. Revenge me.

ORESTES

Come back with me. Come back. Come home.
Trap the imagination of the people.
For you, they'd even turn on Rome.
Be wronged. Be beautiful. Be silent.
Be the bombshell of Berlin,
falling on the Capitol, the Spanish Steps, the Forum,
until Vittorio gives in.
The Pantheon, the Farnese Palace, St Peter's.

IRA

I want revenge. I want it now.
Not next year. I'm hungry for it, ravenous.
And so? So you suggest we plough
the fields and scatter and harvest in six months' time.
You'd say that we should sink a well
if I were dying of thirst. Would you like to know
the exact temperature of hell?
I'm a thermometer one degree away from melting,
that's all. So try to understand
that a war would take too long if it lasted a week.
I will not bend to him. Your hand.
Give me your hand now. Yes. It's a good, strong

hand.
I like the way the fingers move
and I want to give them a little present.
First this,

(*She puts his hand on her body.*)

now this. You disapprove?

ORESTES
This is English. SAS. Black tungsten. What for?

IRA
It's bigger than your other knife,
that Swiss army thing you sermonize over.
Use it today to take a life
and I'll give those lovely hands another present.

ORESTES
Whose life did you . . .

IRA
Vittorio.
In the basilica. Stab him in the face.

ORESTES
I can't.

IRA
There's still an hour to go
before the wedding. Organize all your men.
There's time. But if that man survives
and comes out into the daylight married to her,
well, then he separates our lives.

ORESTES
And you and I have no future together?
Ira, it's too dishonourable:
instead of a war, a dirty little murder.
What's more, the king's invulnerable.
There's his personal bodyguard. Don't forget them.

IRA
He doesn't think about the threat
to himself. They're guarding Angus in case
you try to get the little get
without any diplomatic niceties.

ORESTES
I'm still a servant of the state
engaged in negotiations with an ally . . .

IRA
I want you to eviscerate
your rival, a man who's insulted me deeply,
and listen to you. Prosing on
about protocol like an embassy clerk.

ORESTES
All right, I'm going . . .

IRA
         . . . going, gone.
When did you sell your soul? You were a man once.
Remember? Nothing frightened you.
But now you think like an insurance policy,
so anxious profit should accrue
with the absolute minimum of risk.
Caution will cost you everything.
I'll be frank with you. For whatever reason –

no matter why – I loved the king.
For political or personal motives.
Who cares? The point is this. I cared.
All my humiliations follow from that
naive mistake and now I'm scared
I won't be able to stop what I started
unless Vittorio is dead.
Oh, I want to hate him, but if he survives
I might forgive the shit instead.
Kill him. Every tomorrow means temptation
as long as . . . as we both shall live.

ORESTES

Then he must die. I'll take his elbow and whisper:
take this, it's all I have to give.
They always go up on their toes. It's the shock.
He'll look as though he's taken short
and struggle for words like a stammerer.
I need to give the plan some thought,
though, and here I am racing to conclusions.
I need some time to brief the men
or we won't leave the basilica alive.
I stab him, but what happens then?
We can't assassinate him there. It won't work.
I'll kill him later, at the feast.
When everyone is drunk, it'll be easy.
They'll never notice when they're pissed.
With luck, he'll loll there looking the worse for drink.
That's if I do it quick enough.
Like that, escape won't present any problems.

IRA

By then he's had her bit of fluff,
fitted in between the wedding and the banquet,
and you're too late to stop the slight

to my feelings and Germany's honour.
Klaus, Klaus, don't wait until tonight.
You forget, I know what Vittorio's like.
Urgent. The bride and groom might skip
their own wedding reception, send some excuse,
because she has him in her grip.
She won't be hungry. She'll be full up. I know
exactly what he likes to do.
And he'll do our things. Our private things with her.
Our words. And he'll pretend they're new,
the bastard. Kill him for me this afternoon.
In church. Before he has the chance
to have her, I want you to have him. With this knife.
Go deep, go deeper, till he pants.
Listen for that straining, constipated grunt
he gives each time you penetrate.
Think of pleasure. Think of me waiting for you.
All warm and wet. Don't hesitate.

ORESTES
Hold on, Ira. This isn't the way to do it.

IRA
Out of my sight. Go on. Get out.
But give me the knife back. I'll do it myself.
You'll never know what love's about,
will you? No wonder I decided to leave you.
You're like a girl compared to him.
A virgin. Tight as a rolled umbrella.
He'd murder people on a whim.
Just like that. Why? Because he felt like it.
Well, now I feel like it. So there.
I bet he'll laugh when he sees me with the knife
because he'll think I wouldn't dare.
But he once taught me a two-handed grip

and how to stab with all my weight.
He'll remember when I strike. Then I'll kill myself.
With you I feel my heart stagnate.
Vittorio hurt it into life. The most
I ever felt with you was stitch.

ORESTES

You're like a fire eating all the oxygen.
You've always taunted me, you bitch.
You can get me to do whatever you want.
I'll kill Vittorio for you,
in the basilica, at the altar rail.
You wait.
(*A gurgle of laughter.*)
        I'll make your screams come true.

IRA

That's what I want. Blood on the red carpet.

(*Exit* ORESTES.)

Scene 4

IRA *and* EBERHARD.

EBERHARD

You're being hasty. Yes, my girl.

IRA

I'm too old for you to nanny me, Eberhard.
Let's let the tragedy unfurl,
shall we? In its own sweet way. How, I don't care.
Frankly, I couldn't give a toss.

EBERHARD
Precious.

IRA
No. I'll never feel precious again.
Even these rings. His.
(*She pushes them off, lets them fall.*)
Clinker. Dross.
Worthless. But, Eberhard, the thing should have
a personal touch, a signature . . .
Catch Orestes. Tell him to tell Vittorio
that Ira ordered him. Make sure.
I'd never forgive myself if he didn't know.

EBERHARD
I'll go if you insist. I will,
but . . . Vittorio. Coming to see you.

IRA
Catch Orestes.
His orders are to wait until
further orders. Don't stand like that. Run.

(IRA *gets down on all fours to retrieve the rings.*)

Scene 5

Enter VITTORIO *and* FENICE.
For the first time, IRA *and* VITTORIO *are on stage together.*
Before either speaks, there is a long silence, during which they
try to control their emotions. In the course of VITTORIO'S
speech, we get a glimpse of their erotic fantasy life.

VITTORIO
Now steady. Steady. Take your time.
There's plenty of time. OK? Just keep calm now.
I'm pleading guilty to the crime.
All right? Feel better? I'm offering no defence.
No mitigating circumstance.
A straight plea of guilty on every count.
I don't deserve a second chance,
even if I actually wanted one. Which I don't.
This won't do any good, I know,
but, Ira, I really am sorry that things
have ended up like this, and so
I just thought that I'd come and . . .

(*She hisses and claws the air with one hand.*)

                                              Easy now.
Easy. And just apologize.
I could be banal. I could say it's no one's fault.

(*More hissing and crouching. They circle each other.*)

I haven't come to lionize.
Don't, Ira. Please don't. There's no meat today.
Big cat. Wild cat. There's nothing left.

(*But he holds out a clenched fist. She mouths it menacingly, then licks it as he speaks.*)

I wanted to do what was best for everyone.
I can't. I'm powerful, not deft
like a politician, and the power I have rules me.
It's time we stopped this bloody game.
I'm going to marry an English Jewess.

(*She bites him hard.*)

Be angry, Ira. Don't be tame.
I can't help myself. I *won't* help myself.
I'm here so you can savage me.

(*He closes his eyes. She makes as if to bite him again, then changes her mind. She gets up, spits on the rings in her hand and throws them at him.*)

IRA

You idiot. We were made for each other.
Think. Close your eyes again and see
what we made of each other for each other.
Yes. You invented me. And I
perverted you. Think. Yes, you remember things.
Sick whims she'll never satisfy,
because you won't be able to bring yourself,
for years, to mention them to her.
And when you do. No, don't shake your head like that.
Yes: somehow, something will occur.
I don't know what. What? What do you want most?
The way she slips a stocking off.
Nothing much. But all those little needs you have
will start again. It's like a cough,
a tickle, that turns into a tumour. And in the end,
at last, you'll have to try to speak.
Eh? Croaking out some unspeakable want you feel,
a red spot burning in one cheek,
unable to turn round and face her. Your wife.
Love, love, she'll make you feel ashamed.
Apologetic. You'll live your life in whispers.
She'll make you feel castrated, tamed.
Look at me. Look at my humiliation.

Vittorio, I promise you
that this is nothing. It's nothing at all
to what you'll soon be going through.
Seeing to yourself in the locked lavatory.
Sick in the head. Awake in bed
all night. Her snore like a model aeroplane.
But none of your libido dead.
When you're varicose with desire, think of me.

VITTORIO

You think you know me and you don't.
I never intended to say this but you've been
provocative, as is your wont.
All right, then, the truth, since you seem so keen.
I didn't come here to offend
you. Quite the opposite, actually.
I wanted, if I could, to mend
our relationship, patch up your injured feelings,
effect some reconciliation
perhaps. To concentrate on the good things,
instead of your humiliation.
You're sexy. Sure. But that's all you are to me,
and I was getting bored by you.
All that, that stuff, was boredom in the bedroom:
Christ, running out of things to do,
dutifully doing our bit for Axis. I'm sorry,
but what we had was nothing much.
You'll soon get over it. Six months at most. The thing
began and ended in the crutch.

IRA

(*Shakes her head. Long pause.*)
You're wrong about that. I'll never get over you.
(*Long pause. Struggle for self-control.*)
I understand you. Perfectly.

I know you. You'd like me to be proud, so I
could melt a little, prettily.
Then we'd be a bit sentimental together,
until you leave me for your bride.
At which point, one last sob. To feed your self-esteem.
I need to blow my nose. No pride.
I have no pride. Only all this snot leaking.
I haven't got a handkerchief,
let alone pride. Keep it. I'll use my sleeve.
O love, I hurt. Beyond belief.
Give me something for the pain. Kiss me better.
You won't. No, I disgust you now.
I'm like something mangled in machinery,
squealing like a slaughtered sow,
and you want me to die so the noise will stop.
You're hardly here, are you? You're there
with her, watching a pulse in the crook of her arm.
I'm glad you had the time to spare.
Thank you for coming. Now, for Christ's sake, go.
She's waiting with her oboe voice
for you. Don't you dare touch me. Don't you dare.
Leave me alone. I'm just a noise.
What is it the spurned woman's supposed to say?
You haven't heard the last of me.
That's it. You'll hear me in the basilica,
screaming from the cemetery.

(*Exit* IRA.)

FENICE

What do you think she intended by that last bit?
A threat of suicide, or what?
Maybe just a personal appearance from the
  graveyard.

It could even be a plot.
No one seems to have seen Orestes lately.

VITTORIO
Annette is waiting. Guard the son.
God knows what she meant. None of it made much sense.

FENICE
(*Poker-faced*)
Except the sex. That sounded fun.

VITTORIO
(*Smiling in spite of himself*)
I wouldn't want to go through all that again.

(*The two men burst out laughing.*)

ACT FIVE

Scene 1

Passo romano by the two guards. Lights up on IRA. *She is lighting one cigarette from the end of another. For the first time, the central playing area is almost as cluttered as the surrounding circle of chaos. There are open suitcases and trunks everywhere.* IRA *is packing. But she is wearing a long evening dress. Her eye make-up is extraordinarily smudged.*

IRA
I've always liked this dress. It feels
slinky. Why haven't I worn it more often?
A shade too long without high heels
and just a bit tight. Well, it's meant to be tight.
Somewhere there should be matching shoes.
(*Rummages, throwing out odd shoes.*)
 The same material. And a little evening bag.
 Hey. Here it is.
(*Holds up the bag, then opens it.*)
  Lipstick. Cachous.
(*Pops one in her mouth. Cups her hand to smell her breath.*)
 What else? That shagreen compact. I'd forgotten
  that.
(*Opens the compact and rubs the mirror on her hip.*)
 Now shall we take a little look?
(*Sets up the compact on top of a trunk and half dances towards and away from it, trying to see herself.*)
 Cha-chacha, cha-cha-chachacha-chaaa. Blast it.
 Too small. Sometimes you want to puke.
 Things. I can't see myself. I can't feel myself.
(*Picks up the compact and examines her face.*)
 Once, I was really beautiful.
 Eyes like burnt-out factory windows now.

The fire inside. Gone cold. Gone dull.
There's no one in there. Is there anybody in there?
I wish I knew. And what I felt.
He's left me like a light on in a room
and nothing changes till I melt:
I feel alive and empty. Can't tell day from night.
What's the weather like outside?
It could be raining. Unsteadily. For a change.
Pouring with sun. I can't decide
anything. No feeling. Whatever it is,
I'm here, I'm in my element.
A live wire that can't feel anything at all.
One moment. Empty. Long. Intent.
What's the time? What time do people get married?
(Looks at her wrist, but she isn't wearing a watch.)
It doesn't matter. Dead by now.
We decided Orestes would do it.
That's right. I can't remember how.
Well, he wasn't very nice to you, was he?
He had his chance. It serves him right.
Where did I put that drink down?
(Looks around for it, not very hard.)

                                        I'm not drunk.
Not quite enough to get me tight
in the bottle. Nearly. But not quite. Two glasses.
It's too late now to change my mind.
Anyway, he changed. Not me. I still love him.
(Pause. Her eyes fill with tears. They spill.)
I wonder whether I can find
those shoes.
(She has real difficulty in enunciating now.)
                They were made to match. Same
material.

(*Enter* EBERHARD.)

What have I done? What have I done?

EBERHARD
Nothing. Had a drink by the look of you.
Not that there was *that* much. Begun
to pack and not got very far with it. That dress,
it suits you. Blondes can get away
with the most funereal colours. Find the shoes,
did you? Or have they gone astray?

IRA
You horrible old bitch. Tell me what happened.

EBERHARD
Nothing. I went. The pair were wed.
You could smell his hair oil from the altar to
the organ loft. The royal head
looked like a salad dressed with mayonnaise.
His tailor doesn't stint the braid
either. Brilliantino, the escapologist.
She was impassive. I'd have stayed
if he hadn't looked so pleased with himself.

IRA
What happened when he saw you there?
Did the smile switch off?

EBERHARD
                    Nothing. He didn't see me.
Princess, princess, the place was bare
as far as he was concerned. Except for her.
She was a miracle for him.
There was nothing else he wanted to see.

Cherubim and seraphim
could have staged a flypast without his noticing.
He's made provision for the waif:
heavily guarded in the fortress with Fenice.
And now he knows the boy is safe,
he's convinced there's nothing to worry about.

IRA

He's dead. What did Orestes say?

EBERHARD

To me? Nothing. He was there, though. Watching.
His men took up the second pew.
I was nearer the entrance.

IRA

                He'll bungle it.
He'll funk it, won't he? Answer, you.

EBERHARD

I can't answer. I honestly don't know.

IRA

He's going to betray me now.
He is, isn't he? I should have done it myself.
It's just another broken vow.
Why do I go on believing these men? Stupid.

EBERHARD

He loves you. Something he can't do
much about, that. But. But there are other things.
So try to see his point of view.
Not difficult. He's a professional soldier.
Therefore, deep down, his mind is trained
and not in the usual academic sense.

Listen. His loyalties are strained
in several different directions.
His instinct tells him to obey
whatever requires the greatest self-sacrifice.
That warrior ethic stuff. OK?
So bumping off Vittorio looks pretty suspect
to him, because he stands to gain
by it. Plus, to him, murder doesn't sound heroic.
You're dealing with a soldier's brain.
Right? Right. The basilica is tactically wrong.
Unsound. Too many variables.
Then there's his portfolio from the Führer.
He feels a hundred different pulls.

IRA

Like someone juggling an accordion. So?
Meanwhile Vittorio escapes,
triumphant; Orestes does nothing. Perfect.
And we pack up tonight and traipse
all the way back to Germany. Bloody perfect.
He couldn't take an order down
for breakfast and execute it correctly.
By now I thought I'd have his crown
in my hands. The velvet dirty. The gold dented.
Orestes. Pah. I should have known.
I should have known I couldn't rely on him.
I should have done it on my own.

EBERHARD

He wasn't wearing a crown. I told you already.

IRA

You irritating . . . All right, why?
What's all this sulky indifference about then?

EBERHARD
Sometimes you make me want to cry.
None of this, none of it, is necessary.
To me, the thing is obvious.
But you don't see it. Why bother explaining?
I wish I were you. All this *fuss*.
Take Orestes. He would do anything for you,
the stupid, stupid, stupid fool.
And probably has. I couldn't bear to see it.
I left. Thanks to you, he's like a ghoul.
Haggard. Twitching. But I can remember him
the way he was when you first met.
Christ, he was so handsome. His looks. His behaviour.
The kind of man you can't forget.
You have, though. No wonder. You've made him ugly.
And you, you're ugly now.

(*They stare at each other wearily, in silence. Enter* ORESTES.)

ORESTES
It's done.

IRA
He's dead?

ORESTES
(*Shakes his head silently, then speaks.*)
I can hardly believe it, you know.
So nervous. But once it was begun,
it worked out better than I'd anticipated.
Except I couldn't stab the king:
there were too many people milling around him.
But let me tell you everything

in the right order, exactly as it happened.
He wasn't bothered. Not a bit.
Even though he could see me there with my men.
His voice was clear and definite.
He handed her the sceptre and made a speech:
he promised to protect the boy,
legitimized the kid's claim to the English throne.
I've never seen such naked joy
in anyone as when he looked at his new wife.
And then he turned and grinned at me.
Not defiant. Friendly. He mouthed, 'Look after Ira.'
I realized immediately
he didn't realize why I was there. Amazing.
Had no idea. Not a thought.
Well, why should he? I wasn't known for treachery.
The boy was guarded in the fort
and, in effect, he'd given you back to me.
To him, it would have seemed absurd
what I was planning. Quite unnecessary.
Pointless. Completely undeserved.
I stabbed him in the vestry. He slapped me on the back
and turned to sign the register.
Ira, I couldn't help liking him somehow.
You should have seen his signature.
It slid right across the page and on to the table.
I was surprised he was surprised,
that it hadn't even occurred to him.
Since I was so preoccupied
with what I was going to do, I thought he'd know.
I wish he had. It felt all wrong.
He was happy. He wanted us to be friends.

IRA

Go to hell where you belong.

ORESTES

You're right. It's stupid to be sentimental.
What's done is done. I've killed a man
and that's that. He killed hundreds in his time.
Thousands. A modern Genghis Khan.
In my position, he would have done the same,
and laughed the way he used to laugh,
so you could see his tonsils and adenoids
in every bloody photograph
we ever put out for Axis propaganda.

IRA

How I despise you. Dirt. You're dirt.
Doing your business on the grave of a dead lion.
You dare to stand there and assert
that Vittorio was some kind of Genghis Khan?
A common murderer like you?
His reputation's safe from libels like that.
The charge is patently untrue.
History will fix his stature, find he was
the chief of all the chiefs of staff.
And envied accordingly. Hence his death: murdered
while he signed his autograph.
Don't look so worried, Klaus. I'm going mad, that's
   all.
It's what you have to do, ignore
the facts, when you want to get out of something.
I made a bad mistake before.
Silly me. Not your fault. I'll take all the blame.
Why did you take me seriously?

ORESTES

Because. Ira, mad people don't say they're mad.
You know you're just as sane as me.

IRA

(*Laughs for some time at this.*)
    I love you, Klaus. You can always make me laugh.
    A joke: how sane are you today?
    Excuse me, while I just go and wash my hands.
    I'll be right back. Why don't you stay
    and make yourself uncomfortable somewhere?

(*Exit* IRA.)

ORESTES

(*Takes out his Swiss army knife.*)
    Designed for every problem life
    can present a man with. All eventualities.
    Less like a mistress than a wife.
    Look: scissors, nail file, corkscrew, blade,
    tin-opener, bottle-opener, screwdriver,
    in stainless steel, precision made.
    Suppose you have a screw loose. Tighten it.
    Suppose you've got a broken heart.
    Now, which would be the correct attachment? Yes.
    You stab it better for a start,
    with this, the biggest, sharpest blade.
(*He folds back the gadgets he doesn't propose to use.*)
    Not this, or this, or this, or this.
    Not even this.
(*He folds away the big blade, too. The lights fail.*)
              Put the light back on. Back on.

(*The emergency generator takes over. A dimmer light from caged bulbs, but plenty of visibility, please. Maybe one red light to suggest emergency.*)

    I haven't had my good-night kiss.

(*Enter* OLDENBURG *and troops.*)

OLDENBURG

Cover the stairs and the corridors. Both of them.
Come on, Klaus. Klaus. It's time to go.
We've had it if we don't get out of here now.
They're cross about Vittorio.
You know how excitable Italians are.
Our blokes have held the palace gates,
but there'll be a tank along in minutes and
I wouldn't like to speculate
what will happen then to that lovely ironwork.
It's time we got a wiggle on.
Would you believe it? The widow's full of pique
now husband number two has gone.
Women. Whatever happened to gratitude, eh?

ORESTES

The princess said she'd be right back.
I should probably wait a bit longer.
I think she had a mild attack.
Nothing serious. Very slight. A bit blue, here,
around the lips. I'd better wait.

OLDENBURG

What the fuck are you on about? Ira's dead.

ORESTES

What's the word? Precipitate.
Don't be so . . . I've forgotten the word again.

OLDENBURG

Ira has committed suicide.
No, don't shake your head. Klaus, I saw it myself.
Frankly, I'm not a bit surprised.
Ira never struck me as the stable type.
I knew her temperament was flawed.

Christ, why else was she dressed in an evening gown?
Let's leave. The stairs are like a morgue.

(ORESTES *sets up a kind of dry crying, exactly like a small baby, and picks up various items of clothing, dropping each in turn. We think he must be looking for a souvenir, something of Ira's to which he is sentimentally attached. The baby wail goes on, until he finds what he is looking for – something silk, perhaps underwear, which he holds close to his face and rubs between finger and thumb in silence. It is some time before he speaks.*)

ORESTES

She's gone. What are you doing, Klaus?
Nothing. Talking to yourself. Talking. Talking.
Because there's no one in the house
and it's quiet now that the noise has stopped,
now that you've shut the baby up.
The baby in your head. Like earache. Unbearable.
Then drinking. Water. From a cup
by the bed. A white kitchen cup. Long ago.
Then dreams. Dreams nothing could surpass:
your mother, waterproofing a slice of bread,
and pouring whiteness in a glass.
Until the sweating woke you up like spiders.
Everywhere. You were on your own.
Screaming and terrified of being touched.
And you were in the dark, alone.

(ORESTES *goes on fingering the silk, soothing himself, and slips his thumb into his mouth.*)